Born in a Stable

Models by Charlotte Stowell

Retold by Jane Price

CANDLE
BOOKS

A long time ago a young woman called Mary lived in a village. One day an angel visited Mary. He had some amazing news. "You are going to have a special baby and you must call him Jesus," said the angel.

Who visited Mary?

Wise men follow the star

Joseph and Mary with Jesus in the manger

The wise men present their gifts to Jesus

King Herod

Published in 2005 by Candle Books
(a publishing imprint of Lion Hudson plc)

Copyright © 2005 Lion Hudson Plc/Tim Dowley & Peter Wyart trading as Three's Company.
Cover and interior illustrations by Charlotte Stowell.
Story retold by Jane Price.

Distributed in the UK by Marston Book Services Ltd, PO Box 269, Abingdon, Oxon OX14 4YN
Distributed in the USA by Kregel Publications, Grand Rapids, Michigan 49501

UK ISBN 1 85985 527 X
USA ISBN 0 8254 7297 0

Worldwide co-edition produced by Lion Hudson plc
Mayfield House, 256 Banbury Road, Oxford OX2 7DH
Tel: +44 (0) 1865 302750   Fax: +44 (0) 1865 302757
Email: coed@lionhudson.com   www.lionhudson.com
Printed in Singapore

Mary was happy because she knew her baby was God's son. She married Joseph who was the carpenter in the village. They spent time getting things ready for the baby.

Who is watching Joseph the carpenter at work?

It was nearly time for Mary's baby to be born, but the Governor of the country wanted to count everybody. This meant that Mary and Joseph had to travel a long way, to Bethlehem.

What is carrying Mary to bethlehem?

Mary was very tired when they arrived in Bethlehem. There were no rooms left at the inn.

The kind innkeeper felt sorry for Mary. He said, "I have a warm stable where you can stay."

Who does Mary and Joseph thank?

Soon afterwards, the baby was born. Mary laid him in a manger. All the animals were pleased to share their stable with Jesus.

What is baby Jesus sleeping in?

Some shepherds were looking after their sheep in the fields near Bethlehem. Suddenly they saw an angel. "Don't be afraid," said the angel. "A special baby has been born in Bethlehem." Then the sky was filled with many angels singing praises to God.

Who does the Angel see?

When the angels had gone, the shepherds decided to see the baby for themselves. They left their sheep and ran down to Bethlehem.

What is this shepherd holding under his arm?

The shepherds found the stable and crowded into the doorway. They were so eager to see the baby! When they went back to their sheep they were very happy. They told everyone they met about baby Jesus.

What other animals are there in the stable?

In a far off country there were some wise men who watched the stars. One night they saw a new star. "It means that a new king has been born," said one of the wise men. "We must go and find him," said another.

How many wise men were there?

The wise men packed their bags and set off on their camels. It was a long, hard journey that took many weeks. They followed the new star all the way to Jerusalem.

How did the wise men travel?

The wise men asked King Herod about the new baby king. Herod was not pleased to hear about another king, but he said "When you find the baby tell me, so that I can worship him, too."

Who did Herod want to find?

Finally, the star led the wise men to Bethlehem. They found Jesus with his mother. They knelt down and gave him expensive gifts of gold, frankincense and myrrh. They knew they had found the new king at last.

What expensive gift did this wise man bring to Jesus?

The complete set of models
handcrafted by Charlotte Stowell and featured in
the pages of *Born in a Stable*